Building Your

MW01593361

GRAND BANKS DORY PLANS

www.FraserWheaton.com
www.SaltRockEntertainment.com
www.DoryPlan.com

Publisher's Catalog-in-Publication data
Fraser Wheaton
Grand Banks Dory Plans / Fraser Wheaton
ISBN: 978-1533013613

The Banker Dory – An Introduction

Fishing off the Grand Banks of Newfoundland has always been a dangerous business, especially so, before the advent of modern navigation and boat building technology.

Grand Banks Fishermen had to rough some of the toughest seas in the world to harvest their living from the sea. They needed the strongest, most seaworthy yet agile boats known to man. They therefore came to rely on one boat; The **Dory**.

The dory is a small flat-bottomed fishing boat with high sides that is narrower aft then she is a front. Seamen swear by the dory's stability and maneuverability. The convenient shape of the dory made it easily stackable on the deck of schooners where they would be piled high during transport to and from the banks.

Once at the banks, fisherman would cast out in these dory's by the dozen to hand-line for codfish. The Dory could cover many miles by oar and/or sail and survive the sudden gales that frequent that area. And the ability of these small vessels to carry the heaviest of loads and still maintain its seaworthiness was astounding.

The Dory fulfilled its role in the Grand Banks Fishery until the 1940's. Today, you have to look hard to see a dory used in the fishery. Although they are still sometimes used as life rafts on some fishing vessels, the most common use today for the dory is simply as a pleasure craft. The dory makes an awesome rowboat. It is light, yet very sturdy in the water. They can also be equipped with a small outboard motor for trolling. Depending on the size of the dory, various engine sizes can be used.

The Dory Plans that follow in this manual are that of a 16 foot Grand Banks Dory. It measures 16' from stem to stern with a 12-foot bottom. The dory will be carefully lapstreak planked with pine planks and have a spruce and birch stem and a solid pine stern. Marine grade caulking and stainless steel screws are used to ensure complete water tightness and long life.

The dory makes an awesome pleasure craft. It represents an era long gone and is simply wonderful to see moored in a quiet harbor or lake. The Grand Banks Dory, you gotta love it.

Building Materials Used

8 pieces of white pine used for planking – 16' x 9" x 5/8"
5 pieces of white pine used for the bottom – 12' x 7" x 1 ¼"
5 pieces of oak used for timbers – 6' x 12" x ¾"
4 pieces of pine used for gunwale casing – 8' x 10" x ¾"
2 pieces of pine used for risings – 8' x 4" x ¾"
2 pieces of pine used for thwarts - 5' x 8" x 1 ¼"
2 pieces of pine used for thwarts – 4' x 8" x 1 ¼"
2 pieces of pine used for counter (transom) – 39" x 8" x 1 ¼"
1 piece of pine used for apron – 3' x 4" x 1 ¼"
1 piece of birch used for stem – 39" x 2 ½" x 2"
4 pieces of pine used for bottom tongue – 12' x 2" x ¼"
1 piece of pine used for counter tongue – 39" x 2" x ¼"
2 piece of pine used for batten – 17' x ½" x 1"
1 piece of pine used for knee braces – 4' x 8" x 1 ¼"
2 pieces of pine used for support posts – 6' x 4" x ¾"
3 pieces of pine used for bottom Runners – 12' x ¾" x 2 ½"
2 pieces of 2x4 used for posting the dory. They need to be as long as necessary to run from our ceiling down to about 13" off the floor.

Tools Used

Electric drill
Handsaw
Minimum 4 wood clamps capable of extending at least 35" and small variety of other clamps
Jigsaw with 1" blade
Measuring tape
Hand plane
12" electric planer if you have it
Electric sander
Hammer
Table Saw and a ¼" adjust dado blade
Skillsaw

Fastening Materials Used

2 lbs of stainless steel screws 1 ¼" long with # 8 head
1 lb of stainless steel screws 1 ½" long with # 8 head
1 lb of stainless steel screws 2" long with # 8 head
½ lb of stainless steel screws 2 ½" long with # 8 head
½ lb of stainless steel screws 1 ¼" long with # 8 head
½ lb of stainless steel screws 5/8" long with # 8 head
6 tubes of marine glue # 920 or # 2000
1 tub of pine wood filler, to cover screw heads.

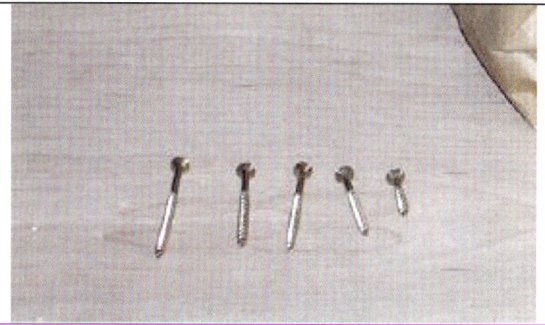

The Beginning and a Word of Advice

Now that you have all of your materials and tools it is time to get stated on our 16' Grand Banks Dory. This is an awesome project that you will be very proud of once completed, and it is a heck of a lot of fun to build. The key with this project, as it is with any building project, is to simply take your time and walk away from it when things just aren't going your way. A few minutes away will clear our head and refocus your attention. That is a lesson we learned the hard way ;-). You will get frustrated on occasion, so walk away and take a breather.

Starting at the Bottom

When building our Dory, we will start at the bottom and work our way up. We must construct the bottom of the Dory first. Pick out the 5 pieces of 12' x 7" x 1 ¼" pine planks that you purchased for the bottom and lay them side by side on a flat work table.

These pieces will be laminated together via a tongue and groove, along with a generous amount of marine glue. The pieces, when fitted properly, will be held together with clamps until the glue hardens. Approximately 24 hours.

Key Point – Using plenty of glue here is important. We don't want water to seep through the joins.

So, you will need to cut a total of 8 grooves. The three inside planks get grooved on each side, while the two outside pieces only get grooved on the inside side. To do that, you will need to setup your table saw with the dado blade adjusted for a ¼" cut width and sitting at 1" high. That setting ensures that you can make your groove cut with one easy pass.

You will turn each plank up on its side, and slide it through your saw blade making one complete pass over the blade. That will cut a 1" groove that is ¼" thick into your plank. With your saw turned off, place a piece of plank on its edge up against the blade and resting against your saw fence. Adjust your fence until you are comfortable that your blade will make the cut in the center of the plank. This is important. The cut should be made in the center of the plank's 5/8" width.

Once your dado blade and saw fence are adjusted correctly, be sure to not adjust it again, otherwise your grooves won't match up and your floor surface will not be even. If that does happen, you will have some sanding on your hands to level it back up. Not fun, but sometimes necessary.

Ok, when you are sure that the blade and fence are correct, it is time to cut the groove. Turn on the table saw and slide the plank over the blade slowly and as evenly as possible until it is cut through the length. This will be our first bottom plank. It only needs to be grooved on one side.

For the next 3 (three) planks, groove both sides. For the 5th and final plank, do as you did with the first plank and only groove one side. This will serve as our end piece.

Now, you are ready to make sure the tongue fits in the groove. Try each piece in the groove where it needs to go to see if they fit snugly. It should be tight enough that it barely fits in the groove. So much so, that you may have to gently tap it in with a hammer.

If either tongue piece is too thick, you can run it through the plainer to thin it out so that it fits the grove. If they fit really loosely, you will need new tongue pieces. It is important that they are not slack in the groove. A tight laminate is important to stop leakage.

Once you are satisfied that each piece fits, apply a bead of glue inside the groove of the first sidepiece. Slide the first tongue piece in the groove. Repeat this process until all 5 pieces are joined together.

Once each piece is fitted, we need to place our 4 clamps on the planks spaced evenly and tighten. Make sure they are tight enough to force the planks together. The glue should squeeze out between the planks.

Let this sit until the glue hardens. Approximately 24 hours.

Take a break. You deserve it!
It is required as part of the instruction manual ;-)

Marking the Bottom

The first step in shaping the bottom is to square off one end. This will be the stern of the boat. If your planks are already square across the end, there is no need to square it off further. If not then proceed with a straight edge of some sort, either a large square or straight board, to mark a straight line across the wood, being careful not to cut too much off. Then, using either your handsaw or a skillsaw cut the end square.

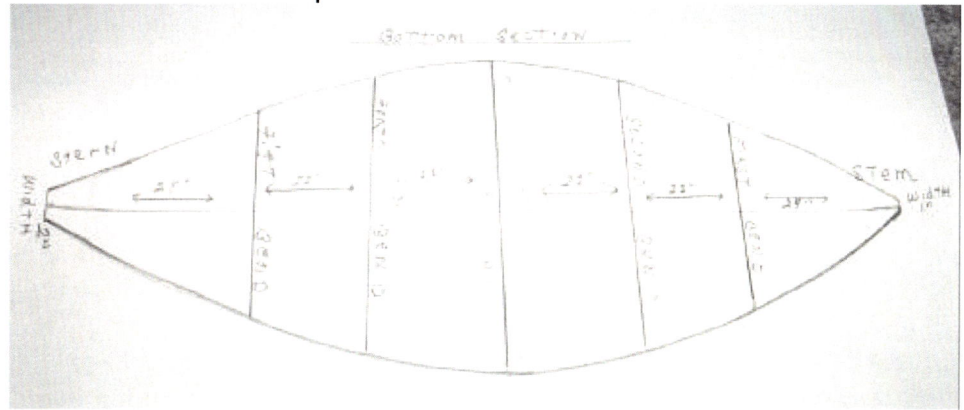

Working from that end, measure up 72". At the 72" point make a mark. This will be the center of our Dory. Using a straight edge, mark a line across the bottom at that point.

From that middle mark, measure back 22" and make another mark, then mark a straight line across the bottom.

From that point, measure back another 22" and mark straight across the bottom.

That should leave 28" between your last mark and the end of the bottom.

Next start at your middle mark and measure forward 22" and make a mark. Then draw a line straight across the bottom.
From that mark, measure another 22" forward and make another mark straight across the bottom.

That should leave 29" between your last mark and the end of the bottom. That end of our bottom will be our stem.

These marks are where our bends of timber will be going. Make sure they are dark enough on your wood to see them.

Now, move up to our middle mark, at the 72" point. The middle of your bottom will be 33" wide. So, measure the width of your bottom at that 72" point. Divide that number by 2, and you get your exact mid point.

Work through that same process at each of your previous marks, and then mark a straight line that runs the entire length of your bottom. That is our center.

Go back again to your middle mark at 72". Your Dory bottom at that mark will be 33" wide. So, measure out from the centerline 16 ½ inches and make a mark. Do the same on the other side. Those side marks are where you will be cutting through when you cut the bottom shape later on.

Next move back to the stern. At that point, your bottom is exactly 2" wide. So measure 1" on either side of our centerline and make a mark.

Then move to the stem. At that point your bottom is only 1" wide. Measure ½" on either side of our centerline and make a mark.

Marking the Dory Shape

Now that we have our bottom marked out for size and timber placement, we will next need to draw out the Dories famous shape. This step is easier then it looks, and is where our 14' ½" x 1" batten comes in.

First, go back to your middle mark at 72", and tack a single 1" nail exactly at our 16-½ inch mark. Just drive it in far enough so that it is firm.

Second, go to the stern. This end is 2". A couple of steps ago we marked a 1" mark on each side of the centerline back here. What you need to do now is to place a 1" nail exactly on that 1"marker. Tack it in so that it is firm. Then, about a ½" inside of that nail, drive in another one in the same manner. The idea here is that our batten will be held in between these two nails and you can mark along its edge.

Next go to the stem. This end is only 1" wide. A couple of steps ago we marked a ½" mark on each side of the centerline up here. What we now need to do is to place a 1" nail exactly at that 1'2 inch marker. Tack it in so that it is firm. Then, at about a ½" inside of that nail, or right at our center marker, drive in another one in the same manner. The idea here is that your batten will be held in between these two nails and you can mark along its edge.

So, what you now have is two nails side by side at the stem, two nails side by side at the stern, and a single nail at the center on your 16 ½" marker.

Now comes the cool part. Take your batten and place it between the two nails at the stem of the boat.

Make sure it is outside our center nail, and follow the bend back along our bottom until you place the batten again right in between the two nails in the stern of your boat.

The batten makes a great shaper as it forms the exact shape of your side.

Our last step for this side is to take our marker pencil and trace along the outside edge of our batten. Make it dark so that you can cut along the edge later.

Once you're done, simply complete the same tasks for the other side as follows:

First, go back to your middle mark at 72", and tack a single 1" nail exactly at our 16-½ inch mark. Just drive it in far enough so that it is firm.

Second, go to the stern. This end is 2". A couple of steps ago we marked a 1" mark on each side of the centerline back here. What you need to do now is to place a 1" nail exactly on that 1"marker. Tack it in so that it is firm. Then, about a ½" inside of that nail drive in another one in the same manner. The idea here is that your batten will be held in between these two nails and you can mark along its edge.

Next go to the stem. This end is only 1" wide. A couple of steps ago we marked a 1/2" mark on each side of the center line up here. What you now need to do is to place a 1" nail exactly at that ½" marker. Tack it in so that it is firm. You should already have your nail right at your center marker, you can use that one this time as well. The idea here is that your batten will be held in between these two nails and you can mark along its edge.

So, what you now have is two nails side by side at the stem, two nails side by side at the stern, and a single nail at the center on your 16 ½" marker.

Once again take your batten and place it between the two nails at the stem of the boat. Make sure it is outside your center nail, and follow the bend back along your bottom until you place the batten again right in between the two nails in the stern of your boat.

Our last step for bottom marking is to take our marker pencil and trace along the outside edge of our batten. Make it dark so that you can cut along the edge shortly.

Our bottom is now completely marked out, and is ready to cut. This is our next step.

This is another great time for another coffee and lunch break.

Sawing the Bottom

We will saw the bottom using our Jigsaw or skillsaw. Saw setup is simple. The bottom sides need a 5/8 inch bevel all the way around so as to match our timbers. So, simply angle your saw base at a 5/8".

We then proceed to cut along the marker line that we traced around our battens. Be careful to keep your saw base flat on the bottom of your boat. The blade is angled, so your base needs to remain flat. Take your time and do not force the saw. Let the saw do the work for you.

Cut one side, and then cut the other. Our bottom is now completed. Laminated, glued, marked, and sawed. Great job so far.

If you had some difficulty in sawing the bottom with the 5/8" bevel, just take your sander and go over it, sanding enough to make it a little smoother and more even. Be careful not to sand too much though. Best just to touch it up a little. The 5/8" bevel is important.

Bottom Supports

You must now place 5 supports across the top of your Dory bottom. The supports will remain in place and help strengthen the bottom of your Dory and will serve as supports for the timbers.

These 5 supports are each 4"wide and ¾" thick. Their length depends on where you place then along the bottom. They should be long enough to almost reach the edges, but not quite as long. Taper the edges as shown in the photos so that they taper back towards the center.

Our first support should be placed in the middle, at our 72" mark. It needs to be placed just behind our 72" mark, so that the front edge of our support is on the line. You should run a bead of glue along the bottom of it, put it in place, and screw it down using (8) 1 ¼" screws as shown.

Our second support goes just behind the second bend mark that we made earlier (remember the 22" marks?) so that the front edge is touching our mark. It gets glued and screwed down the same as the middle support using 6 or 8 screws.

The third support goes just behind the third mark that you made earlier. As with the others, it goes so that the front edge is touching our mark. It gets glued and screwed down just the same as the middle and second support using 6 screws.

Our fourth support this time goes behind the middle support. It goes at the 22" mark we made running back towards the stern. It too goes just behind the line so that the front edge is on the line. It gets glued and screwed down just the same as the middle and second support using 6 or 8 screws.

The fifth and final support gets placed on the last 22" towards the stern of the Dory. Just like the others, it gets placed just behind the line so that the front edge is on the line. It gets glued and screwed down just the same as the middle and second support using 6 screws.

Your finished bottom should look similar to this (Minus the upright beams of course…They come later):

Posting Your Dory.

It is very important that your Dory is 2 inches lower in the center then she is at either end. That rocker shape is enforced early on and maintained by a set of floor blocks and posts.

You can do this any way you chose, but we use the setup above. Our front and rear floor blocks are setup to be 15" off the floor, while our center block is 2" shorter at 13". We keep our blocks securely in place with a couple of angle brackets screwed to the floor as the picture above shows.

It is not enough to have the floor blocks lower in the center. You also need a way to force the floor of the Dory down into this rocker shape. We do this as is noted in the picture above. We use two 2x4 posts that lay on top of the front and aft bottom supports and are actually posted up into a ceiling beam. The posts are long enough so that in order to fit between the Dory floor and the ceiling beam, they have to be jammed in place. That forces the floor down into shape against the floor blocks as shown.

Constructing the Counter (Transom)

Constructing the counter is remarkably similar to building the Dory bottom. It involves laminating several pieces of pine together via glue and a tongue and groove method.

Pick out the 2 pieces of 39" x 8" x 1¼" pine that you purchased for the transom. Lay them flat on our worktable. Those two pieces need to get laminated together just like you did when you constructed the bottom.

To do that, we will need to setup our table saw with the dado blade adjusted for a ¼" cut width and sitting at 1" high. That setting ensures that you can make our groove cut with one easy pass.

We will turn each plank up on its side, and slide it through our saw blade making one complete pass over the blade. That will cut a 1" groove that is ¼" thick into our plank. With our saw turned off, place a piece of plank on its edge up against the blade and resting against our saw fence. Adjust our fence until you are comfortable that the blade will make the cut in the center of the plank. This is important. The cut should be made in the center of the plank's 5/8" width.

Once our dado blade and saw fence are adjusted correctly, be sure to not adjust it again, otherwise our grooves won't match up and our floor surface will not be even. If that does happen, we will have some sanding on our hands to level it back up. Not fun, but sometimes necessary.

Ok, when you are sure that the blade and fence are correct, it is time to cut the groove. Turn on the table saw and slide the plank over the blade slowly and as evenly as possible until it is cut through the length. This will be our first transom plank. It only needs to be grooved on one side.

Repeat this process exactly for the next plank, grooving only one side.

Now, we are ready to make sure the tongue fits in the groove. Try the tongue piece in the groove where it needs to go to see if they fit snugly. It should be tight enough that it barely fits in the groove. So much so, that you may have to gently tap it in with a hammer.

If the tongue piece is too thick, you can run it through the planer to thin it out so that it fits the grove. If they fit really loosely, you will need a new tongue piece. It is important that they are not slack in the groove. A tight laminate is important to stop leakage.

Once you are satisfied that the tongue piece fits, apply a bead of glue inside the groove of the first sidepiece. Slide the tongue piece into the groove. Repeat this process with the second plank and slide it over the tongue half that is protruding from our first plank. Square up the two pieces so that the top and bottom edges are square. This is important to eliminate having to square it off later and cutting our planks.

Once the pieces are fitted, place 3 or 4 clamps on the planks spaced evenly and tighten. Make sure they are tight enough to force the planks together. A little glue should squeeze out between the planks.

Marking the Counter (Transom)

Now that our counter is dry and laminated, you can remove the clamps and mark out the shape with our pencil marker.

The transom is 2" wide at the bottom, and 14" wide at the top, with a 3" round above that. At the highest point, the transom is 38", but is only 35" at each side.

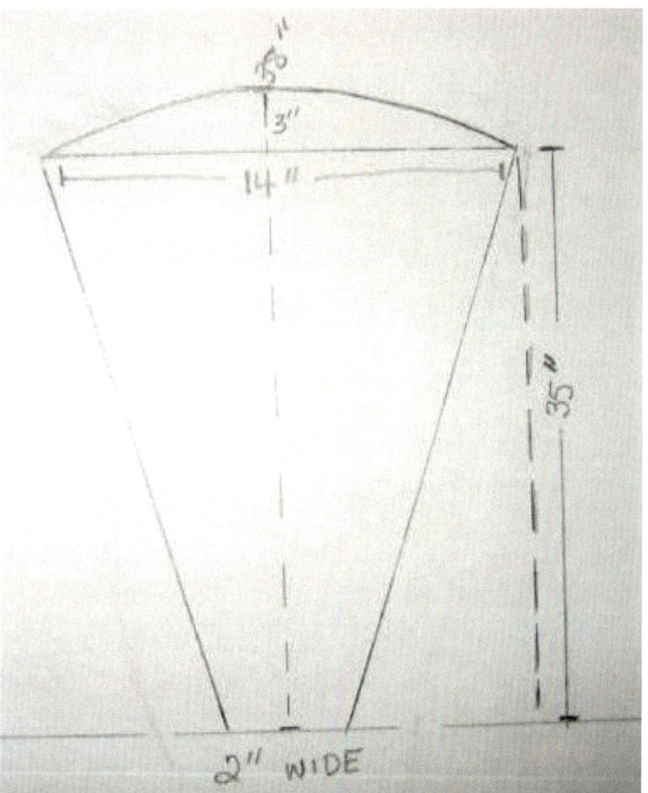

The following illustration shows the dimensions:
Please use this diagram to mark out our transom. Notice that the maximum height of our transom is 38", and that is only at the center. The true height is 35" at the sides. The 3" rounded topper accounts for the additional height.

The transom is 14" wide at its widest point. That tapers down to 2" wide at the bottom. That 2" is the same width as the aft of our Dory bottom.

Once we have our counter marked out and you are satisfied, we can cut it out using our Jigsaw or skillsaw.

Both sides of our counter and the counter bottom need the same 5/8" bevel that we used for our Bottom. Our planks wrap around and screw into the sides of our transom, so it follows that it cannot be square. The counter sides must have the 5/8" bevel as the boat bottom to allow the planks to wrap around.

The counter bottom needs the 5/8" bevel so it fits snuggly against the bottom of our boat and the knee brace that holds it in place.

Congratulations. You just completed our transom. Now to make and mount our counter knee and stem knee braces.

Making and installing our Knee Braces – The Stern Brace

The counter will get solidly held into place with a stern knee brace. That brace is made from pine and is 12" along the bottom, and 12" up the back. It is cut at a 132-degree angle. That will create the 24" rake for the stern.

Draw our brace out from the 4' piece of pine you purchased for the braces, using the measurements above. The plank will not be wide enough to draw out the brace flat across, but you can draw it out on an angle.

We can use our Jigsaw to cut it out and do the rounding on the top. We make ours as shown, and suggest you use a similar pattern. Once you have it cut, sand it so as to remove splinters and rough edges.

Once you are satisfied with it, run a bead of glue along the bottom edge and stick it into place. Then screw it down to our Dory bottom with two screws. We use a 3" screw at the end, and a 4" screw closer to the middle of the brace. Screw them in on a slight angle for maximum grip.

Making and installing our Knee Braces – The Stem Brace

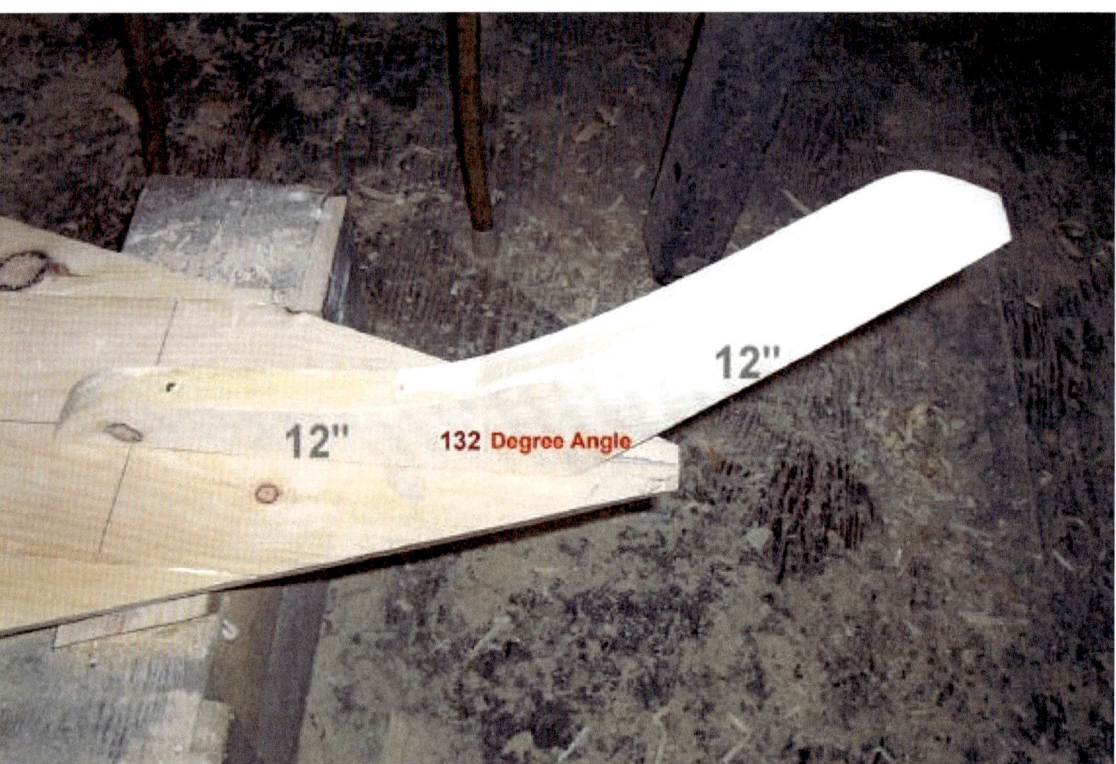

The stem brace is in fact, an exact copy of the stern brace. It is 12" along the bottom, 12" up the front, and has a 132-degree angle. That will create the 24" rake for the stem as well.

Draw the brace out from a solid piece of pine using the measurements above. We can use our Jigsaw to cut it out and do the rounding on the top. We make ours as shown, and suggest you use a similar pattern. Once you have it cut, sand it so as to remove splinters and rough edges.

Once you are satisfied with it, run a bead of glue along the bottom edge and stick it into place. Then screw it down to our Dory bottom with two screws. We use a 3" screw at the end, and a 4" screw closer to the middle of the brace. Screw them in on a slight angle for maximum grip.

Our completed stem brace should look as shown above. Congratulations on another job well done.

Fasten the Counter

Ok, so we have a counter that is ready to go. We also have a counter brace that is mounted and ready. Lets go ahead and fasten the counter onto the stern brace.

This process is a matter of using plenty of glue. Put a generous bead of glue along the back of the knee brace and down on the bottom of our counter. Slide the counter in position as indicated in the above picture. Fit it exactly center so that our 2" counter bottom is square with the edges of our floor.

We then fasten the counter to the knee brace by using a 3" screw about an inch down from the tip of the knee brace that goes through the brace and into the counter on a bit of a downward angle. Then drill a 4" screw through the brace and into the counter a few inches further down, in the same manner.

With both screws be sure to place them where they will actually go through the brace and into the counter without going through the back end of the counter. It is important not to drive the screw out through the counter. If you do that, you will need to take the screw out and fill the hole with plenty of marine glue, and start over.

If you notice our photo shows a green trimmed piece of wood across the counter. That is simply a temporary brace that we tacked into the counter and the wall, just to keep the counter in place while the glue hardens. You can put a chair up against the counter if you want, or use a brace like we did. You might just need something to help the counter stay in place while the glue dries.

Crafting our Apron

The apron fastens directly to our stem brace in a similar manner as our counter. It relies on a generous amount of glue, a 3" screw and a 4" screw.

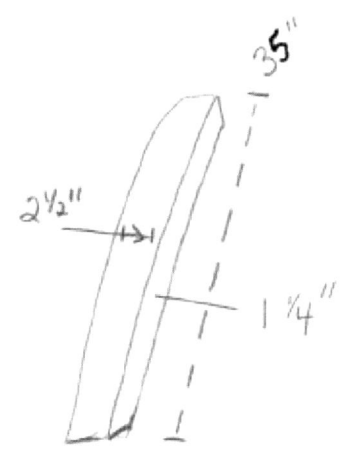

1/2" Bevel on each side of your apron

The apron measurements are as follows: It has a total length of 35", which if you remember is also the height of our transom. The apron is 2 ½" wide, and 1 ¼" thick. The key to a successful apron is the ½" bevel it needs on both sides. You simply set our Jigsaw on ½" bevel when you cut it out from our plank.

Pick out the 3' x 4" x 1 ¼" piece of pine you purchased for the apron. It is already the appropriate thickness, but is about an inch too long, and too wide.

First make a mark about a quarter of an inch in from one edge. Do that on the top and bottom, and then use a straight edge to connect the marks.

Then make sure the bottom end is square at 36". Measure from the top end, down 35", and make a mark along the entire width.

Now we will need to cut our 1/2 " bevel along the side and the bottom of our apron. The top is ok as it is. This process is the same as with the bottom and the counter. Set the Jigsaw or skillsaw angle at ½" and simply cut along our bottom mark. Then cut along the length mark all the way along the length of the piece.

Next, measure the piece at 2 ½" wide and make a mark. Do that at the top of the piece, and again at the bottom. With your straight edge, mark a straight line joining the two marks. That is the width of our apron.

Using our Jigsaw or skillsaw with the ½" bevel again, cut all the way along that mark.

Now we have a finished apron, and it is now ready to fasten to our stem brace.

Fasten our Apron

Our apron goes fastened in the same manner as the counter. Run a generous bead of glue along the edge of our stem brace and along the bottom of our apron. Slide the apron firmly into place in the center of our stem brace. You will then need to secure it there with two screws. A 3" screw near the top of the brace, and a 4" screw nearer the center. Screw them in on a slight angle and make sure they do not protrude through our apron.

The Timbers

The timbers are made from oak and form the ribs of our Dory. Solid timbers are crucial to a sturdy long lasting boat.

For our purposes, the timbers will be constructed in 3 separate pieces. Those pieces will be glued and fastened together with screws to form the U shaped bend as shown in the picture above.

From here on I will refer to one of these complete U pieces as a bend. A bend of timber will mean the entire U that runs down one side, along the bottom and up the other side.

Our 16' Dory will have 5 bends of timber. (The above photo only shows 3). They are 22" apart and placed at the lines we drew earlier. Each bend will rest against a support plank as the above photo indicates.

Each timber is the same size and shape. The only difference is the amount of bevel on each bend. We will get into that a little later.

For know though, let's get into marking out and cutting our first bend; the middle one that sits at our 72" mark. It is the easiest one because it has no bevel.

Draw and Cut The Middle Bend Timbers

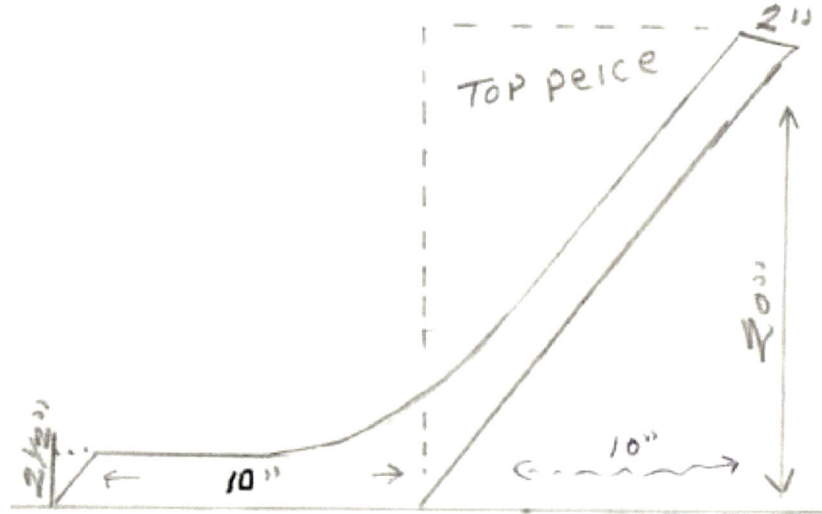

The Middle bend is composed of the two side timbers and a joining middle U shaped bend. The middle timbers have no bevel so we will start with this one.

Pick out one of the oak pieces you bought for the timbers and lay it flat on a worktable. We need to draw out a timber exactly as shown above.

On the bottom edge we need to measure 20" and make a mark. Also make a mark at the 10" point as well.

From our 20" mark, measure up 20" and make a mark. Using a straight edge, connect our 10" mark with our 20" mark on the top.

From our 20" mark, measure out to the left 2". That is the top thickness of our timber.

From the bottom starting point of our timber, measure straight up 2 ½". Our timber is a full ½" thicker on the bottom, then it is on the top.

Now simply mark free hand along the top of our bottom half, turn up the bend of our timber and continue to mark up to the top of our timber. What you have now is a shape similar to a hockey stick, and resembles what you see on the drawing above.

Now, let's take our Jigsaw, without a bevel, and cut out our timber. Once you have it cut, lay it flat against our oak and trace it out. Once traced, cut that one out with the Jigsaw as well.

Sand both pieces until edges are smooth. You now have the two side timbers for the middle of our Dory.

Cut for water drainage

Before going any further, you need to trim the corner of the timber so that once it is in place water can freely run down along the sides of our boat.

We simply take our handsaw and cut the corner away. Maybe a 1" trim like the photo here.

Note that in this photo, the bottom of the timber is not cut off on an angle at the tip. It is simply pushed down into a hole in the table saw.

Install the Middle Bend Timbers

Ok, now we will install the middle timbers, one on each side at our 72" mark. Do so as shown in this picture. The key here is that they rest up against the middle support board that you installed at the 72" mark.

Run a bead of glue along the edge of the support board and lay the timber up against it. The outer edge of the timber should be out to where it forms an even line with the bevel on the outside edge of our Dory bottom.

Secure it to the support with (3) 1 ¼" screws.

Do the exact same process on the other side of the dory. The timber should be slid out so that it forms an even line from the top all the way down to the dory bottom. Remember, that our plank has to be secured up against the dory bottom, and the timber.

Draw, Cut, and Install the Middle Join Timber

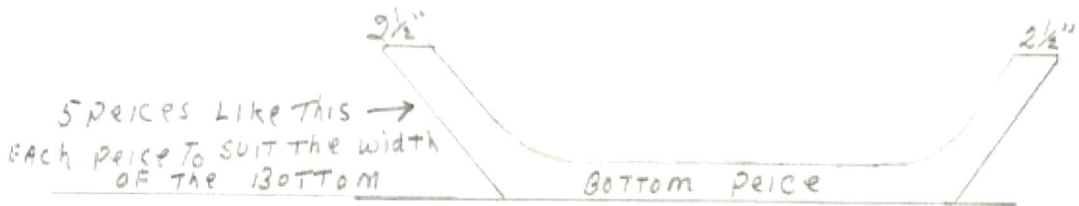

This piece of oak will run along the bottom of our dory and turn up each side of our timber. It actually goes in front of the two timbers you just set in place, and fastens to them with glue and screws.

This piece is of a different length for each bend, depending on where it is in the Dory. It depends on how wide our dory is at that given location.

For the middle bend, the bottom of our Dory is 33" wide. Therefore this piece needs to be 33" wide as well. So it is 33" wide along the bottom, then it will turn up 6". At each top, the timber is 2 ½" wide as the diagram indicates.

Using freehand, you can draw out the inner side of the timber, making sure the inside corners are rounded somewhat.

Using our Jigsaw, saw out the bend, and then sand it so that the edges are smooth. Just like the timber pieces earlier, you will need to trim the outer corners so that water will flow freely down the Dory sides. If you want, you can lay this piece in place, and just mark out the corner cuts so it matches the timber pieces that are already secured in place, then cut them with a handsaw.

Run a good bead of glue along the back of this timber piece and stick it in place against the front edge of our timber arms. Then screw it in place with (4) 2" screws.

Ok, one completed timber bend down, 4 more to go!

The Remaining Timbers

The remaining timbers are just the same as the middle ones in size, shape and installation except for one key factor; the bevel that we need to cut along the outer edge.

Our planks will wrap around these timbers from back to front, so it follows that each timber will need to have a bevel cut in it to allow the plank to wrap around it evenly.

The next set of timber arms you will cut will be placed in front of the middle bend, 22" in front to be exact. It gets screwed into the support plank that we screwed down into the bottom, 22" in front of the middle bend.

These timber arms are the same size and shape as the middle ones except that the outer edge has to be cut with a 1/16" bevel that tilts forward. The plank will start at the aft end of our Dory and run forward. It will rest against the middle timber that has no bevel, but then start to bend forward towards the stem. Each timber that sits in front of the middle timber will need a bevel that allows the plank to wrap forward; in this case 1/16".

So, mark these timbers exactly as we did with the middle two, but when we cut them out, use a 1/16" bevel on just the outside edge.
Once they are cut, remember to trim an inch off the outside corner for water drainage along the side of the Dory, just as we did with the middle bend. When they are cut and sanded, glue and screw them in place as with the middle bend.

 Once these timbers are in place, you may want to temporarily brace them as we have done in this photo.

This bend of timber needs the bottom U shaped bend as well. It is exactly like the one you cut for the middle, except it is shorter. Once our timber arms are in place, measure the width of our dory at that point. That is how long this timber bend needs to be cut.

Mark and saw it out just as you did with the middle bend, sand it, glue it, and screw it into place.

Our last forward bend of timber is the same as the previous bend, except that this one needs a ¼" bevel along the outer edge to allow for the plank to wrap around towards the stem.

Mark these two timbers as before, but when you cut the outside edge, make sure our Jigsaw has a ¼" bevel.

Once they have been cut out, sand them and be sure to cut off an inch at the outside corner to allow for water drainage.

Glue and screw them into place just as before, with the outside edge forming an even line down to the bevel of our Dory bottom.

This bend of timber needs the bottom U shaped bend as well. It is exactly like the one you cut for the last bend, except it is shorter. Once our timber arms are in place, measure the width of our dory at that point. That is how long this timber bend needs to be cut.

Mark and saw it out just as you did with the middle bend, sand it, glue it, and screw it into place.

Now, we will need to install the two bends of timber that sit aft of the middle bend. This process is like the process of installing the two bends that sit in front of the middle bend, except the bevel gets cut in the opposite direction.

Our plank starts off at the stern and wraps immediately out towards the middle of our Dory. Therefore the bevel will need to be slanted towards the stern of the boat. If you stand at mid-ship and look aft, the bevel is slanted towards the counter.

The first aft timber gets a 1/16" bevel like the first fore timber did, just in a different direction. You draw the timber out exactly as before, but when you cut it, cut it with our Jigsaw on a perfect straight angle, just cut it a little wider then it should be; maybe a ¼". Once it is cut, simply bevel our Jigsaw to 1 1/16", turn our timber over and trim off the excess ¼" with the saw using the bevel. That will bevel our timber in the correct direction.

Do the same with the second timber arm. Trim away an inch from both outside corners to allow for water drainage, sand and put it into place against the front of the support plank with glue and our screws, just as we have been doing.

Once those are in place, measure the bottom of our Dory at that point where our bottom bend needs to go. That width will be the length of the bottom bend.

Draw out that bend just as before, only using the appropriate length to fit this bend. Cut away an inch for water drainage, sane and fasten in place with glue and screws as before.

Now for our last bend of timber. Mark it out and cut the two timber arms exactly like we did for the last set, except they get a ¼" bevel. That ¼" bevel matches the bevel on our foremost bend of timber.

Then fasten the timbers in place with glue and our screws.

Measure the width of the Dory bottom at that point where the bottom bend needs to go. That width will be the length of our bottom bend.

Mark, cut and secure this piece in the same manner as you have done the previous 4.

Take a break. You just completed a lot of work, and should be proud. This is the point where we stop for a breather and make sure everything you have done to date looks and feels right. You should do the same. Let our timbers set securely into place before proceeding.

Welcome to the world of Battens

Remember that piece of pine you have that is 18' x ½" x 1". Time to get it out. If you simply cannot get a piece this long, you can join two pieces together. Just be sure that one of our pieces is at least 14' long, and that when you join them, it still provides a straight edge. Notice in the photo below, we had to join ours to get the full length.

Battens are used to shape our Dory on top, before you put our planks on. The reason we have them so thin, at ¼" is so that it bends easily and is quick to go into shape.

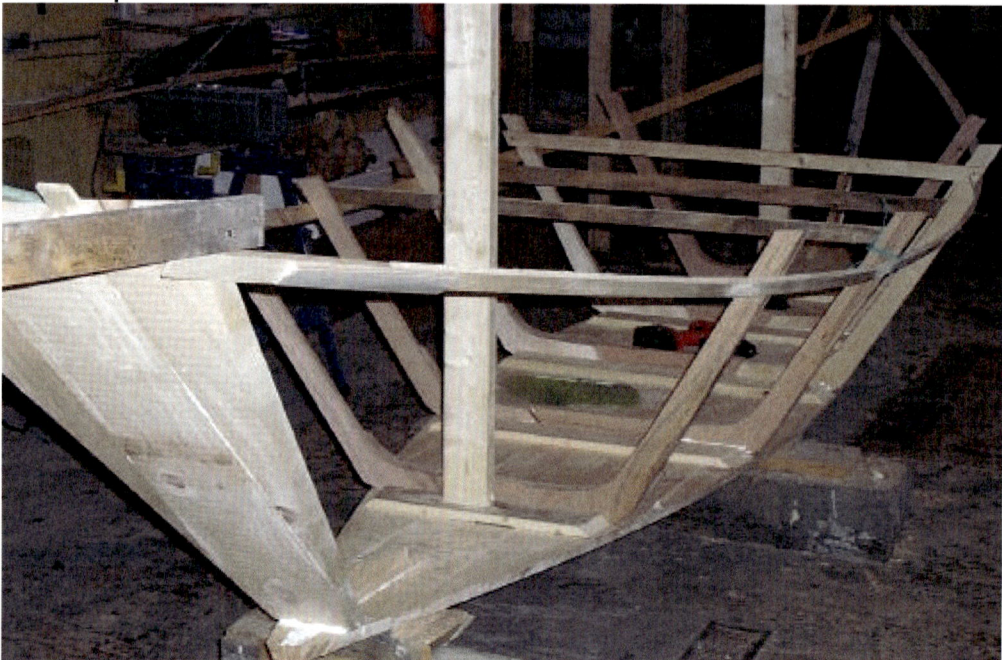

Start at the counter when installing the batten. Our counter will be 35" high, so start by marking our beveled counter edge at 35" from the Dory bottom.

Then secure our batten to the counter edge with a 1 ¼" screw. Make sure the TOP edge of our batten is exactly at the 35" mark.

Our Dory will be 20" high at the middle bend. So, mark our middle timber at exactly 20" up from the Dory bottom. For this mark, DO NOT measure up on the angle of our timber, but instead measure straight up from the bottom. Secure the batten at the middle bend with a 1 ¼" screw, so that the TOP of our batten is exactly at the 20" mark you just made.

Our Dory will be 35" high at the stem. Make a mark on the side of the apron at exactly 35" from the Dory bottom.

Secure our batten to the apron so that the TOP of the batten is exactly at the 35" mark.

Walk back and forth along the side of our dory and slightly adjust the batten up or down on the unscrewed timbers, then stand behind the Dory and look up along the batten. Do this until you are satisfied that the batten runs along the Dory in a manner that you are pleased with. This line will be the top of our Dory, so it is important that it runs smoothly.

Now, perform the exact same exercise on the other side of the Dory. It is very important that once you are completed, you have exactly the same measurements on both sides of our Dory. Both battens must be identical in height on both sides of our timber bend.

Once you are absolutely sure both battens are perfectly in place, take the marker pencil and mark each timber along the bottom edge of the batten. Do this on both sides of our Dory.

Congratulations. You have just outlined the top of our Dory.

Beveling The Planks

The most fun part of this whole Dory building process is planking our Dory. It will add shape to our creation and give you a great feel for how the final product will shape up.

Bottom or Garboard Plank. Bevel on one side only

2nd plank, bevel on both sides

Notice the 2" bevel

3rd plank, bevel on both sides

Pick out 4 of our pine planks at 16' x 10" x 5/8". It will take 4 of these to plank one side of our Dory. Each plank has a 2" bevel on at least one side. The planks will overlap each other by 2".

The bottom plank, which we will call the garboard strake, has a 2" bevel on only one side. The non-beveled side goes on the bottom, with the bevel on the top, ready for the next plank to overlap it. Lets measure and cut this one first.

Place one plank flat on a table or workspace. Measure back from the edge 2" at one end and make a mark. At various points, say 3' apart do the same thing. Once you reach the other end, use a straightedge and connect all the marks. That will draw our even 2" line. Our bevel will start at that line and go to a point right out to the edge.

There are several ways you can cut this bevel.
- ?? If you have a large table saw capable of cutting a 2" bevel, then by all means set our blade so that it will trim out a full 2" to the end of our plank, and run our first plank through the saw.
- ?? You can also take this bevel off manually with a hand plane, or electric hand plane. This method is closer to how it was done in the old days, but

requires a lot of elbow grease. It is fun though to do it this way if you have the nerve for it.

?? You can also use a small axe to trim our plank out to a point all the way along its 16' length. This takes a steady hand and a lot of patience as well, but it can be done. Be careful not to cut away the ends though. That will cause you to ruin the whole plank.

?? Another option is to setup a 2" beveled block in an electric planer and slide the planks through several times until it trims the edge 2". It will take some figuring out, but we have done it and it works ok after several passes.

?? Of course, you always have the option of bringing our plank back to the lumberyard where you bought it, and having them cut if for you. Most lumber supply stores these days will cut your lumber for you when you buy it there, if you ask them.

However you decide to trim the bevel, the garboard strake only needs beveling on one edge.

Our second plank needs to get beveled on both sides. Just like the plank in the above photo indicates. You will need to mark and bevel one side, turn it over and do the same on the other side. This plank needs to fit the bevel of our garboard strake, and have the other side beveled as well, so our third plank fits into it.

Our third plank is exactly like our second one. It needs to get beveled on both sides. Just like the plank in the above photo indicates. You will need to mark and bevel one side, turn it over and do the same on the other side. This plank needs to fit the bevel of our second strake, and have the other side beveled as well, so our fourth plank fits into it.

Our fourth and final plank only gets a 2" bevel on one side. In that manner it is like our garboard plank. Measure and mark one side at 2". Then use our beveling method of choice to trim out the edge.

You can sand the planks once all 4 are cut. That will help the overlapping process go easier, and will produce a much nicer looking Dory once you are done.

Now that you are done, start all over from scratch and perform that exact same process with the 4 planks remaining for our other side. Just duplicate each step you just did. When we start planking, we will do both sides at once. One plank on one side, then switch to the other side and do the same.

Once you get all 8 planks beveled, you can proceed.

Planking Our Dory

Ok, lets install our garboard plank first. Before we glue it into place, take some time to look at how it goes up against the bottom of our Dory, and rests against the timbers. It will go all the way down to where it is level with the underside of the bottom of our dory, so that it completely covers the bevel of our bottom. The square end goes down, with the bevel facing upwards.

Once you see in your mind how this plank goes on, we can start installing it. The planks go on at the stem first, and we wind our way back. You will need 4 clamps for this process.

The planks go on and are fastened, and then you will cut each end to match the angle of our stem and stern. Expect some to hang over on each end for now.

First you will need to apply a generous bead of glue along the bottom 8 or 9 inches of our apron, each plank, the counter, and all along the Bottom bevel of the Dory floor. Plenty of glue here is key. We do not want any leaks once this is done.

Once our glue is applied, we will fasten the plank to our apron with (2) 1 ¼" screws, one on top and one on bottom. You may need someone to help hold the plank level and in place, or you can let the back end of the plank rest on a block of wood or low stool.

Once the plank has been attached to the apron, without too much wastage (leave just enough of a overhang to saw), bend the plank back to our first bend of timber and clamp it in place. Don't screw it, just clamp it fairly tightly where you think it needs to go. Then move back to the middle bend of timber and slowly clamp it there as well. Clamp the plank to the timber tight enough so that it doesn't slide around.

Next move back to the last bend of timber and clamp our plank there as well.

Finally, clamp our plank at the counter, in the position where it needs to be. Now is our chance to make any adjustments on this plank. Take a long look at each bend of timber to make sure that the plank is down to the bottom of the boat floor and level with the underside of it. Also check to make sure that the plank fits each timber well. You may have to loosen a couple of clamps and adjust the plank accordingly.

Once you are satisfied with the way the garboard plank looks, you can start screwing the plank into our timbers and Dory floor. Use the 1 ¼" screws and place 2 screws at each bend of timber. One on the bottom of the plank that goes straight into the Dory floor, and one that is just under our bevel mark. You can remove clamps as you go. When you reach the counter, screw the plank directly into the edge of our counter.

Now, in between each bend of timber, place two screws into the bottom of our plank and into the floor spaced evenly apart. Do that all along the bottom.

Once our garboard plank has been fastened, take our handsaw and saw off the excess at the stem and stern.

Saw it on the same angle as the counter and stem, and as close to them as you possibly can without sawing into the apron or transom.

Now that this garboard strake is secured on one side, do the exact same thing on the other side. Be sure to use plenty of glue and slowly bend our planks into each timber, clamping as you go.

Congratulations, you have just put on our first strake of plank. Stop, enjoy our success, have a cup of tea or coffee. We always do!

Ok, now it is time for strake number 2. The good news is this strake goes on pretty much the same as the last one, except that it is beveled on both sides. When you clamp it in place and secure it to the stem, make sure that the bottom bevel slides down and completely covers the bevel of our garboard plank. These planks need to completely overlap at the bevel.

So, apply a generous bead of glue all along the bevel of our garboard plank that is already fastened. Notice in the picture below, glue actually squeezes out between the planks when you clamp and screw them together. Use enough glue for that to happen. Once that is done, simply repeat the planking process in the same manner as before. You fasten the plank to the apron, then clamp as you go until you reach the stern, and clamp the plank to the counter. Once it is in place, make sure to adjust it so that the garboard bevel is covered snuggly by the bevel of our new plank.

Once our satisfied with it, fasten it into place. This time use the 1 ¼" screws, but only fasten at the timbers, using 2 screws at each timber, one on top of the plank, just below the bevel line, and one on the bottom of the plank. Do that all the way back, removing clamps as you go.

Now that both planks are fastened at the timbers, take out your 5/8" screws and place two screws, set evenly apart, between each timber and between the last timber and the counter, and the first timber and the apron. Screw them into the bevel where our two planks just joined. These short screws serve to bind our planks together. This is in addition to the glue you placed on the bevel.

So, our two planks are now fastened to the apron, the timbers, the counter, and each other.

With a handsaw, trim off the excess on each end as you did with the last plank.

Then repeat the entire process on the other side of the Dory.

Outstanding, strake number 2 completed!

You're in luck. The third strake is exactly like the second one. Our plank is beveled on both sides. You successfully fastened the second strake, so no reason why you should have any issues with number three either. Just follow the same process as with the second plank, exactly step by step, and on both sides of our Dory. Here is how our Dory should look after the 3rd strake has been successfully attached:

Our boat is really taking shape now as you are close to finishing the planking. The fourth and final plank is a little trickier. This plank will be referred to as the shear plank. As this photo indicates, we will not need all 9" of the plank to fill in the space between our 3rd plank and our batten.

The shear plank is only beveled on one side, and the bevel goes on the bottom, pressed against the bevel of the third plank. When you trim this plank, trim down from the top.

Ok, if you have not yet done so, mark a dark line along each timber at the top of the batten. Also mark the apron and counter at the top of our batten as well. That mark is where the top of our forth plank will need to be. Then you can remove your batten.

Now we must figure out the width of the shear plank at the apron, each timber and our counter.

First measure the distance down from the top of our apron down to the beginning of the bevel on our third plank. Include the bevel in our measurement because the shear plank will overlap it. That is the width of our shear plank at the apron, so mark the plank at the same width where it will fasten to the apron.

Measure distance, including bevel.

Next measure the distance from our apron, back to the first bend of timber. Then measure off the same distance on our fourth plank, and make a mark. Now, at that first bend of timber, measure the distance down from our mark, to the third plank, including the bevel like you did at the apron.

Whatever that distance is, measure it straight down from the first timber mark you just made on the shear plank. That is the width of our shear plank at our first timber.

Repeat this process all the way back at each timber and at our counter. Measure the distance to the next timber and make a mark on our plank at the same distance. Then measure the distance from our batten mark down to our third plank, including bevel. Then follow up with making the same distance mark straight down from the timber mark you made on our plank.

Once our shear plank has been marked, you simply need to connect the marks that you have made from one end of our plank, to the other end. Now take our Jigsaw, skillsaw, or handsaw and saw along that mark, all the way along our plank.

Once we finish sawing we usually take out a hand plane and run along the top edge we just cut. That will smooth away and rough edge and or bumps.

Repeat that process for the shear plank on the other side of our Dory until it too is cut out and planed if necessary.

The good news is that in dealing with the shear plank, the most difficult work has been done. You have them cut. Installing them is exactly the same as you have done with our other planks. You run a generous bead of glue along the apron edge, the counter edge, and the third plank bevel and on the timbers. Then you fasten the plank in place at the apron and clamp our way back.

Once you are satisfied that it is in place where you want it, you can secure it to our boat with the 1 ¼" screws and to the third plank with the 5/8" screws.

Do that for both sides and WE ARE DONE planking our Dory.

Finally, you will need to take our handsaw, and trim off the tops of each timber. Cut them straight across at the height of our top plank, like in the photo above.

Next we will move on to installing our Risings.

Installing the Risings

Here in Newfoundland we simply call em risins, by dropping the g sound. You can call them what you want, but they get installed next. Risings run along the partial length of our Dory along the timbers. Our thwarts will eventually get installed on top of these planks.

Pick out your two pieces of 8' x 4" x ¾" pine that was purchased for risings. Also pick out our 1 ½" screws. They will be used to fasten the risings to the timbers.

Our rising runs along our timbers at exactly 7" below each timber top. So, start by measuring 7" down from the top of each timber and making a mark. That mark will be where the top of our rising will be.

Once they are all marked, run a small bead of glue starting at our mark and running down about 4".

The rising will get screwed to the timbers but at 8' long it will reach further then from timber to timber. It will extend about 3" or 4" past the last timber and the first timber as the image above shows. Push the rising in place and fasten it to the timbers with the 1 ½" screws. Place two screws in each timber, one at the top and one at the bottom.

Repeat the process for the other side. Both risings should now be installed.

Installing the Thwarts

Our seats, or thwarts get installed next. You will be making four of them, from the 4 pieces of pine planks you purchased for the thwarts.
2 pieces at 4' x 8" x 1 ¼" and 2 pieces at 5' x 8" x 1 ¼".

Pay close attention to the above photo, displaying the thwart configuration. Notice that the aft most thwart looks like it is notched into a timber like structure. That is not a timber, but just a support board you will install later.

For now, lets focus only on the longest thwart. It sits not at our middle bend of timber, but at the bend that is forward of it. It is notched out so that it fits into the timbers and sits on the rising.

To get our exact measurement, you will need to take our tape and measure the width of our Dory at the exact point of that timber, from dory side to dory side.

The thwart needs a 5/8" bevel so that it fits our Dory side. Using our Jigsaw with a 5/8" bevel, or if you have a sliding compound miter saw that can bevel at that angle, cut one end of our 5' thwart boards with that bevel.

Next measure off the width that our thwart needs to be, and mark it there. Now cut it off with our 5/8" beveling method as well.

That thwart needs to now get notched out to fit our timber. So, measure the width and thickness of our timber, and mark out our notch on the end of our thwart. Try to make sure the notch it in the mid point.

You can use a handsaw or jigsaw to cut each of the side marks back, and then use a chisel to break away the end piece.

Once completed, do the same thing for the other end. Measure, mark and saw. Then, apply a bead of glue inside the notch and on each end, and snap the thwart down in place. Using 2" screws, fasten your thwart to the rising, two screws on each end of the thwart.

Our next thwart will go aft of the one you just installed. It goes immediately behind our second last bend of timber. You do not need to notch this one.

Simply measure the distance from side to side at the exact point behind that timber bend. Then, at about 8" further back, measure the width again. Because our Dory is narrower at the stern, the ends of our thwart are not square. Mark out the lengths on each side of one of our thwart boards. When you cut it out, make sure that both ends have the 5/8" bevel.

Place a bead of glue on each end, and lay our thwart down in position. Using 2" screws, fasten it to the rising, two screws on each end of the thwart.

Our third thwart will involve some additional work, but is based on the same idea. It is the thwart that goes just in front of our counter.

From the image above, it looks as if it is notched into a timber. That is not the case. It actually sits on top of a support board, and then another vertical board sits on top of our thwart, giving the impression that the thwart has been notched.

First we will need to put the support posts in place. They are 32" up in from of the counter. So, measure up 32" from our counter and make a mark. Do that for both sides. That is where our support posts will go.

At that 32" point, measure up from the floor to the top of our planks. That height is the height of our support posts. Cut them out from one of the pieces of 6' x 4" x ¾ pine you purchased for that purpose.

Once you have both of them cut at the perfect length, measure 7" from one end, draw a straight line across the board at that point, and cut it off square. Do the same for the second piece. Do not throw away the 7" pieces. They will go on top of our thwart.

Run a good bead of glue along the back of the support piece. Place it up against the side of our dory at the 32" mark you made. Secure it in place with 1" stainless steel screws, screwed in from the outside of our dory and into our support. Use 4 screws.

Do the same for the other support post.

Now, we will measure, cut and install a thwart that will rest on top of those posts. Measure the width of our Dory at 2" forward of our support post, then at 2" behind our post. Our posts are 4" wide, while the thwart is 8" wide. Approx. 2" will stick out on each side of the post. Because our Dory is narrower at the stern, the ends of our thwart are not square. Mark out the lengths on each side of one of our thwart boards. When you cut it out, make sure that both ends have the 5/8" bevel.

Place a bead of glue on each end, and lay our thwart down in position. Using 2" screws, fasten our thwart to the support post, two screws on each end of the thwart.

Measure the distance now from our thwart to the top of our plank. Now take those 7" pieces you cut earlier and cut those to the same length.

Apply a bead of glue along the backs of then, and place them on top of our thwart so that from a distance it looks as if the thwart is notched into the support post. Once in place, secure them to the side of the dory with 1" screws that are screwed in from the outside of the Dory and into the support post.

Ok, you now have three thwarts in place. Only one more left. This thwart is created and secured in the same manner as the last thwart you installed. It rests on top of newly installed support posts.

This thwart gets installed on top of support posts that sit at 38" from the stem.

At that 38" point, measure up from the floor to the top of our planks. That height is the height of our support posts. Cut them out from one of the pieces of 6' x 4" x ¾ pine you purchased for that purpose.

Once you have both of them cut at the perfect length, measure 7" from one end, draw a straight line across the board at that point, and cut it off square. Do the same for the second piece. Do not throw away the 7" pieces. They will go on top of our thwart.

Run a good bead of glue along the back of the support piece. Place it up against the side of our dory at the 38" mark you made. Secure it in place with 1" stainless steel screws, screwed in from the outside of our dory and into our support. Use 4 screws.

Do the same for the other support post.

Now, we will measure, cut and install a thwart that will rest on top of those posts. Measure the width of the Dory at 2" forward of our support post, then at 2" behind our post. Our posts are 4" wide, while the thwart is 8" wide. Approx. 2" will stick out on each side of the post. Because our Dory is narrower at the stem, the ends of our thwart are not square. Mark out the lengths on each side of one of our

thwart boards. When you cut it out, make sure that both ends have the 5/8"
bevel.

Place a bead of glue on each end, and lay our thwart down in position. Using 2"
screws, fasten it to the support post, two screws on each end of the thwart.

Measure the distance now from the thwart to the top of our plank. Now take
those 7" pieces you cut earlier and cut those to the same length.

Apply a bead of glue along the backs of them, and place them on top of the
thwart so that from a distance it looks as if the thwart is notched into the support
post. Once in place, secure them to the side of the dory with 1" screws that are
screwed in from the outside of the Dory and into the support post.

Congratulations are in order once again my friend. We have installed our thwarts!

Gunwale Support Blocks

The next step in our building process is to install support blocks between our timbers, and at the stem and stern. A couple of these blocks will also support our rowlocks.

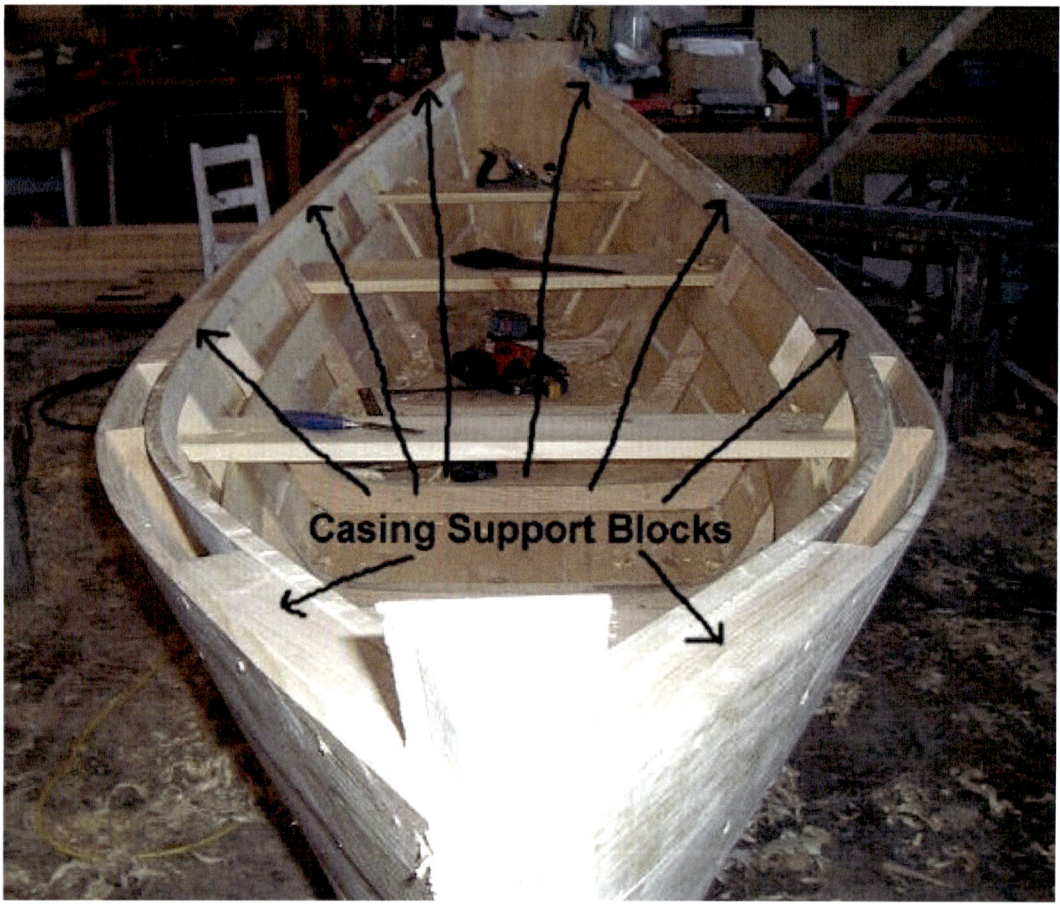

Casing Support Blocks

This image shows the support blocks in place, as well as the inside casing. For now, we will focus our attention on the support blocks only.

Al blocks are 2" wide and 1 ¼" deep. The blocks that extend back from the stem on each side are 2' long. The blocks that extend from the counter are 2' long as well. There are a total of four blocks (2 on each side) as well that fit between the timbers. Those will be the length of the distance between the timbers. You will need to measure that to get the exact measurement.

These blocks go flush with the top edge of our top plank. Simply put a good bead of glue on the edge that sticks to the sides of the dory and squeeze them in place. Then fasten them to the sides of the Dory with 1 ¼" screws, that get screwed in from the outside and extend into our blocks.

Secure each one just as the above picture indicates.

Inside Casing

The inside casing is a strip of pine that is a total of approx. 17' x 2" x ¾". It is very difficult to purchase 17' long pine, so we suggested buying 2 pieces at 9' long. You can join them at a timber, or at one of our support blocks to get our total length.

The inside casing runs parallel to the side of our Dory, for the entire length. Both sides come to a point at the stem.

Here is an example of how the inside casing joins at the stem:

So, you can mount the inside casing all the way around the inside of our Dory, so that it sits flush with tour newly installed blocks.

It is easier to start this process at the stem and follow it all the way back.

Apply a good amount of glue to the sides of our blocks and timbers and screw the casing on using our 1 ¼" screws.

Once our inside casing is in place, you can move on to installing our gunwale casing.

The Gunwale Casing

The gunwale casing can be a little tricky. We will have to take our time with this step and think about what we need to accomplish. Spend some time looking at the pictures that are included in this section.

The casing goes on in 4 pieces. In the stern it is notched for the counter and in the stem, it is cut so that the two sides join.

Pick out the 4 pieces of 8' x 10" x ¾" pine that you purchased for the casing.

The casing is 3" wide at the stem and stern, and 4" wide that the mid ship bend. The idea of using 10" board is that we have to place the plank on top of our gunwale and trace underneath it to get the curvature of our Dory. The plank has to start out that wide in order to have enough board width to cut the bend of the Dory as it wraps around.

We will install the casing at the stern first. Place our 8' plank on top of our gunwale and slide it back until it hits the counter. Slide it as far in towards the center of the Dory as you can and still have it covering the outer edge of our topside.

Next take your marker pencil and mark up underneath the board all along the outer edge of our dory for the entire length. Once it is marked, take it off, turn it upside down and using our jigsaw, saw along our mark.

Then, put the board back in place so that the edge you just cut is flush with the outer edge of our dory all along the board.

At the counter our casing is 3" wide, but at the middle of our Dory, the casing is 4" wide.

Key Point - When it is in place, the casing will have an even overhang inside the dory and out

So, at the counter, slide our casing out so it has a 3" overhang and clamp it down in place.

At the other end of our plank, slide it out so that it has a 4" overhang, and clamp it in place there as well.

Now we can mark out the inside curvature. With our marker pencil up underneath our board, trace along the inside of the dory all the way along the plank.

Take off the board, turn it over and use the jigsaw to cut along our line.

So far, so good. Now you will need to notch out the casing so it fits back along our counter. Take your time here because we can easily cut it incorrectly and spoil the casing.

The counter is 1 ¼" thick, so our notch needs to be 1 ¼" deep on the outside. The cut across our plank cannot be straight, because the sides do not run straight up our dory. The notch needs to be cut on an angle. If you have a bevel handy, you can use it to get the angle of our counter corner, and then cut our casing on that angle. If we put our casing in place, slid back to our counter with an even overhang inside and out, you can see where our notch cut needs to begin.

Once the cut is made, slide the casing back into place and make any adjustments so that it fits snug.

The other side of our dory should be identical to this side, so you can actually just take the casing you just cut and use it to trace out our second piece on our second casing plank. Lay it on top of our fresh plank, trace it out and cut it using a jigsaw.

We now have our two stern casings. You can apply a generous amount of glue to the bottom of each and secure them in place with 1 ¾" screws. Screw the casing down through the top and into the support blocks.

Now we will measure, cut and install the casings at the stem.

These get installed via the same process as the stern casings. It is 3" wide at the stem and 4" wide at the middle.

The casing gets notched at the stem as well, so that it extends up past the apron. You can notch this out by free hand, or by using a bevel to get the angle of your apron, then cutting the same angle into your notch. You can also use a piece of cardboard to practice cutting your notch into. Once you have the right cut into your cardboard, you can trace it into your casing.

We prefer to use a bevel. Simply take the angle of the apron with the bevel, and transfer that same angle into your casing as a notch. Of course, you also have the option of NOT notching the casing. Simply slide it up to the apron, and later cut a small piece to fit in along the side of the apron. Screw it down and use wood filler to make it look seamless.

Place your plank over the railing and measure and cut them in the same manner as with the stern casings. The two stem casings meet in the middle, so you will have to cut off the inside corner on a straight angle so they meet.

Here is an example of how they meet in the middle.

Once the front casings have been cut, you will most likely need to square off the other end so that it joins the stern casing that is already in place. Make the two casing pieces join flush, then glue and screw the casings in place.

Well, another milestone completed. Our casings have been successfully installed. Once you have had a well-deserved break, we will continue on with our last major step; the birch stem.

The Stem

Our stem is made from solid birch and is what will protect our dory from the front. With its snug fit and beveled edges, it will look as if it is part of the entire stem piece once we have it installed.

The stem measures 39" long, is 2" wide and 2" thick. It is birch and has a 1" bevel along each of the two sides. This bevel can be cut with our jigsaw or table saw.

Once we have our stem cut to the above measurements, it is time to put it in place. Apply a generous amount of glue along the back of the stem piece and along the apron. The stem piece bevels forward, so apply it with the bevel facing towards you.
Once you have the stem in place, fasten it to the apron with (5) of the 3" screws, spaced evenly apart.

This image was taken later in the process with the dory upside down, but it gives a good example of how the stem fits the front of our apron.

Glue will squeeze out along our edges. You can wipe it to help fill in our gaps.

A little later on, you can also use wood filler around our stem to fill in any necessary spaces and gaps. The several coats of paint will protect the filler.

The Oarlocks

Oarlocks are purchased in two pieces. One piece gets cut into our gunwale and the other simply slides into a predrilled hole. The oarlocks get placed, and the whole drilled 1-foot stern of our thwart. That distance is perfect for reaching forward and rowing. As luck would have it, there is also a support block there for you to drill down into.

You will be rowing from your widest thwart, so measure a foot back from the widest thwart on each side. Then, drill a 1" hole straight down through our gunwale and into the support block. Next, it is a simple matter of placing the oarlock plate on top of the gunwale so the holes line up, and tracing around the sides of the plate with our marker pencil. The gunwale will need to be cut down inside this mark so the plate fits into it.

Once it is traced, you can use a chisel to notch out the rectangle shape, just deep enough for the plate to sit in it flush with the gunwale.

Repeat the process for the other side.

Fit the plates into the hole, and screw them down using screws that came with our package.

Congratulations! We have completed most of our woodworking!

Pine Wood Filler

Ok, it is now safe to say that the bulk of our woodworking is indeed over. Now is a good time to break out our pine wood filler, and fill in all of our screw heads, and any crack or chip that you think needs filling in. Exactly where you apply the filler is up to you, as long as you get each screw hole as a minimum.

Take your time with this process and be sure to fill in all of our screw holes inside our dory, on our gunwales and casing, and outside as well. Be generous with the wood filler. You will sand it all smooth a little later on.

Turn Your Dory Over

Our next step will be to install our bottom runners. For that, you will need to turn our dory completely upside down.

The Bottom Runners

These supports are needed to ensure the protection of the dory bottom. Anyone who intends to ever beach their dory will especially appreciate their usefulness.

These bottom runners run the length of our Dory and are approx 10" apart.

They are ¾" x 2 ½" x the bottom length.

Measure the length of our bottom at the center and cut the first runner 2" short of that length. Once cut, place a heavy bead of glue along the back of it, and put it in place at the center of our bottom. Screw it in place with 1 ½" screws, placed 6" apart.

You will now need to place runners that are approx 10" on each side of our center runner. So, measure to the left of our center, 10" and make a mark on the bottom. Then measure the length of our dory at that mark. Cut your second runner 2" short of that length, then attach it to the bottom of the dory in exactly the same manner as before.

Next, measure to the right of our center, 10" and make a mark on the bottom. Then measure the length of our dory at that mark. Cut your third runner 2" short of that length, and then attach it to the bottom of the dory in exactly the same manner as before.

Now, our runners are installed.

Sanding Your Dory

Our last step before painting our Dory is to give her a quick sanding on the outside of our planks. This will smooth any roughness in the wood, and smooth our wood filler over the screw heads.

Using medium grit sandpaper, give the outside of our dory a quick once over to smooth everything out. Any rough spots, or spots with excessive filler need extra attention. Stop once you are satisfied with the surface of the plank.

Our next step is to paint our Dory. We will do that after I grab a coffee ;-)

Painting the Bottom

We will use two colors of marine grade Dory paint. The bottom up to water line, gunwales, and thwart trim get painted with 3 coats of Marine Green. The planks, and the inside get 3 coats of Dory Buff Yellow paint.

We will paint our bottom and water line first. Before we can paint correctly, we will have to mark our water line.

Luckily for us, that is easy because our water line runs along the bottom edge of our second plank. So, our garboard plank and the bottom get 3 coats of green paint.

Apply a coat, let it dry and apply the second coat. Once coat number two dries, apply the third and final coat.

Painting the Planks

The sides of the Dory get 3 coats of Dory Buff Yellow paint.

Notice that the tip of our stem does not get painted yellow. It goes painted green.

Apply one generous coat of yellow. Once it dries apply a second, and then a third once the second coat dries.
Once our yellow has dried completely, we can turn our dory over and paint the topsides. Our gunwale, stem head and thwart trim get 3 coats of green, while the rest of the inside gets 3 coats of yellow.

This image shows a dory with the counter cutout for an outboard engine. Ours will have a solid counter as per the plans.

This image also has a cuddy storage compartment in the front. It shows as green. Ours will not have this unless you add it yourself later.

Trimming the Thwarts

The trim on our thwarts gets painted green. You can create the shape by using a common compass from a geometry set, a divider, or simply by hand. At the peak, the trim is 7" out from the side of the dory.

Then thwart trim gets 3 coats as well.

Congratulations. We have completed our 16' Grand Banks Dory. You should be proud. It has been a lot of work. Well worth it though as we look at our completed Dory.

I truly hope you have enjoyed building your Dory as much as we have, and that you have found our plans helpful.

Take Care and God Bless

Fraser & Wilbert

Made in the USA
Lexington, KY
03 September 2018